LET'S
see

Farm Life

by Jennifer Blizin Gillis

Content Adviser: Susan Thompson, Agriculture Communications,
College of Agriculture, Iowa State University

Reading Adviser: Rosemary Palmer, Ph.D.,
Department of Literacy, College of Education,
Boise State University

Let's See Library
Compass Point Books
Minneapolis, Minnesota

Special thanks to Nu Horizons Farm, Pittsboro, N.C.; Manco Farms Inc., Pittsboro, N.C.; and Matzah Rising Farm, Alamance County, N.C. — JBG

Compass Point Books
3109 West 50th Street, #115
Minneapolis, MN 55410

Visit Compass Point Books on the Internet at *www.compasspointbooks.com*
or e-mail your request to *custserv@compasspointbooks.com*

On the cover: A teenage girl holds a prize-winning lamb.

Photographs ©: Peter Beck/Corbis, cover; Richard Hamilton Smith, 4, 8, 14; The Image Finders/Bruce Leighty, 6; Unicorn Stock Photos/Alice M. Prescott, 10; U.S. Department of Agriculture/Ken Hammond, 12; Kevin R. Morris/Corbis, 16; Unicorn Stock Photos/Nancy Ferguson, 18; Creatas, 20.

Creative Director: Terri Foley
Managing Editor: Catherine Neitge
Editors: Brenda Haugen and Christianne Jones
Photo Researcher: Marcie C. Spence
Designers: Melissa Kes and Jaime Martens
Educational Consultant: Diane Smolinski

Library of Congress Cataloging-in-Publication Data
Gillis, Jennifer Blizin, 1950-
  Farm life / by Jennifer B. Gillis.
      p. cm. — (Let's see)
Includes index.
ISBN 0-7565-0673-5 (hardcover)
  1. Farm life—Juvenile literature. I. Title. II. Series.
  S519.G539 2004
  630—dc22   2003028295

$14.65

630
GIL
c. 1

Table of Contents

NOTE: In this book, words that are defined in the glossary
are in **bold** the first time they appear in the text.

Life on a Farm

Farms are found outside of towns. They have lots of room to raise crops or animals. Many farmers raise both.

Some farms are not very large. They may be less than 100 acres (40 hectares). Other farms can be hundreds of acres. An acre is about the size of a football field including one end zone.

Farmers live in farmhouses with their families. The farm also may have houses or trailers in which hired workers live. Some workers may come only at **harvest** time. There is lots of work to do at harvest time, and farmers often can use some extra help.

◄ *A farm near Spring Valley, Wisconsin*

Farm Buildings

Farms have special buildings. Some buildings, such as barns, may hold animals. There may be separate buildings for chickens and pigs.

On **dairy** farms, the **milking parlor** is an important building. It is where dairy cows are milked. The milk is kept in the milking parlor until the **milk tanker** comes to get it.

There are special buildings for keeping **grain.** A silo is a tall building where grains such as wheat or oats are stored. Farmers also may use smaller, round metal buildings to store their grain. These buildings are called bins.

◄ *Corn is stored in bins.*

Waking Up

There is so much work to do on a farm that farmers must get up very early.

On dairy farms, farmers usually milk the cows early in the morning and again late in the day.

In the summer, it is cooler early in the morning than it is in the afternoon. Many farmers feed and take care of their animals while it is still dark. This way, they can work in their fields before it gets too hot.

◄ *A farmer stands on his porch as the sun comes up.*

Chores

Farm children help with jobs around the farm. These are called chores.

On dairy farms, children may help clean equipment in the milking parlor. This keeps germs from getting into the milk. The children help feed and take care of the farm animals.

Farm children help with chores in the fields, too. They often learn to drive tractors when they are young. The tractors pull different farm machines in the fields. Farm children also help harvest crops.

◄ *A boy feeds a sheep.*

Feeding the Animals

Animals usually eat two times a day. Farmers feed them early in the morning and again in the evening.

If there are just a few animals, farmers may feed them by hand. They shovel feed into **troughs** for pigs and cows. They fill feeders for chickens and other farm birds.

On farms with a lot of animals, farmers grind up corn, soybeans, oats, and other grains in machines called mills. Then the farmers use tractors to pull the mills to the animals' pens and empty the food into troughs.

◄ *A man helps a farmer feed the sheep on her Montana ranch.*

Field Work

In the spring, farmers get their fields ready to plant. Sometimes they pull plows through their fields with tractors to mix up the soil. They may use tractors to pull **discs** through the field. The discs chop up parts of old plants. Then farmers can plant seeds for a new crop.

While the crops are growing, farmers must watch them carefully. Every day, they make sure that insects are not eating the crops. They keep weeds away from the growing plants.

In late summer, the crops are ready to harvest. Farmers work quickly to pick the crops. Sometimes farmers work late into the night.

◄ *A Minnesota farmer harvests corn late in the evening.*

Barn Work

There is a lot of work to do in the animals' pens and barns. Some farm animals live in stalls. They are smaller areas inside barns or other farm buildings where animals are kept. Farmers and farm workers must shovel **manure** out of the stalls. Then they put the manure on the fields to help crops grow.

Farmers spread straw on the floors of the stalls. This makes a kind of bed for the animals. After a few days, they shovel out the old straw and put in fresh straw.

◄ *Horses in a stall*

Caring for the Animals

Farmers must be a little like **veterinarians.** They watch their animals closely to see if any are hurt or sick. If an animal is not too sick, a farmer can give it shots or medicine without calling a veterinarian for help.

Many new animals are born in the spring. It is a very busy time for farmers. Sometimes they must help animals **give birth.** Then they must make sure the baby animals are healthy. They give them vitamins. Sometimes they trim the animals' teeth to keep them from biting one another.

◄ *A man feeds a calf from a big bottle.*

From the Farm to You

Most farmers raise animals or crops to sell for food or other **products.** When animals are fully grown, a truck takes them to be sold. Farmers get paid by the pound for these animals.

Farmers sell some crops, such as corn or oats, to companies that make cereals, oil, or other products. Trucks take the grain to a grain **elevator.** It is stored there before being shipped to **processing plants.**

Some farmers sell crops they raise at farmers' markets. There, you can buy fruit or vegetables directly from the farmers who grew them.

◄ A man pays for items he wants at a farmers' market.

Glossary

dairy—relating to milk cows and milk products

discs—farm machines with very sharp, round metal pieces that can chop up tough parts of old plants

elevator—a big building used for storing grain from many farmers

give birth—to have a baby

grain—seeds from plants such as corn, wheat, oats, or barley

harvest—to gather crops

manure—animal waste

milk tanker—a truck with a special tank that keeps milk clean and cool

milking parlor—a place where cows are milked and where milk is stored on a farm

processing plants—places where crops are treated, or changed, to get them ready for people to eat

products—things that are made or manufactured

soil—a mixture of broken-up rocks and rotting plant and animal material

troughs—long, low containers used for feeding animals

veterinarians—doctors who take care of animals

Did You Know?

• Round bales of hay weigh thousands of pounds. They are moved one at a time by a tractor with a forklift and are stored outside. When winter comes, a few bales are moved into a field for cows to eat. Square bales of hay are smaller and weigh less. Farmers can lift them without using machines. Square bales are stored in barns or sheds to use for animal food and for bedding in stalls.

• Many farmers form groups called cooperatives (co-ops). These groups help farmers save money by buying seed and fertilizer in large amounts, which makes them cheaper. Farmers in co-ops also work together to sell their grain and animals. Sometimes co-ops buy expensive farm machines that everyone in the group takes turns using.

Want to Know More?

In the Library

Geisert, Bonnie. *Haystack.* Boston: Houghton Mifflin, 1995.

Longenecker, Theresa. *Who Grows Up on the Farm? A Book About Farm Animals and Their Offspring.* Minneapolis: Picture Window Books, 2003.

Wilkes, Angela. *A Farm Through Time.* New York: Dorling Kindersley, 2001.

Wolfman, Judy. *Life on a Pig Farm.* Minneapolis: Carolrhoda Books Inc., 2002.

On the Web

For more information on *farm life*, use FactHound to track down Web sites related to this book.

1. Go to *www.facthound.com*
2. Type in a search word related to this book or this book ID: 0756506735.
3. Click on the *Fetch It* button.

Your trusty FactHound will fetch the best Web sites for you!

On the Road

Garst Farm Resort
1390 Highway 141
Coon Rapids, IA 50058
712/684-2964
To see cows and buffalo, go horseback riding, or ride on a draft horse wagon

Long Acre Farms
1342 Eddy Road
Macedon, NY 14502
315/986-7730
To visit a cornfield maze and have fun at farm festivals

Index

About the Author
Jennifer Blizin Gillis writes poetry and nonfiction books for children. She lives on a former dairy farm in Pittsboro, North Carolina, with her husband, a dog, and a cat. She is more of a gardener than a farmer, but has lived on farms and in farming communities.

ABB-2070